My Birthday Party

Sharon Coan

Publishing Credits

Rachelle Cracchiolo, M.S.Ed., *Publisher*
Conni Medina, M.A.Ed., *Managing Editor*
Jamey Acosta, *Content Developer*
Dona Herweck Rice, *Series Developer*
Robin Erickson, *Multimedia Designer*

Image Credits: p.3 ©iStock.com/Samuel Locke; pp.3, 12, Back cover ©iStock.com/Ruth Black; pp.4, 6, 8, 12 ©iStock.com/Rawpixel Ltd.; pp.4, 12 ©iStock.com/ktaylororg; p.7 ©iStock.com/misha_ru; p.11 ©iStock.com/tacojim; all other images from Shutterstock.

Library of Congress Cataloging-in-Publication Data

Coan, Sharon, author.
My birthday party / Sharon Coan.
pages cm
Summary: "How do you plan for a birthday party? Knowing more, less, and equal will help you know what to do."-- Provided by publisher.
Audience: K to grade 3
ISBN 978-1-4938-2063-4 (pbk.)
1. Arithmetic--Juvenile literature. 2. Birthday parties--Miscellanea--Juvenile literature. I. Title.
QA115.C63 2016
513.2'1--dc23

2015011982

Teacher Created Materials
5301 Oceanus Drive
Huntington Beach, CA 92649-1030
http://www.tcmpub.com

ISBN 978-1-4938-2063-4

Printed in Malaysia
THU001.48806

March
Sunday Monday Tuesday Wednesday Thursday Friday Saturday
1 2 3 4 5
6 7 8 9 10 11 12
13 14 15 16 17 18
20 21 22 23 24 25
27 28 29 30 31

birthday

6 friends

equal

6 friends

less

6 friends

more

6 friends

equal

Words to Know

birthday

equal

friends